# Joan of Arc

*Joan of Arc, waving her sword and banner overhead,*
*rallies the French troops at the siege of Orleans.*

# Joan of Arc

## TRACY CHRISTOPHER

## CHELSEA JUNIORS

a division of CHELSEA HOUSE PUBLISHERS

Chelsea House Publishers

EDITORIAL DIRECTOR    Richard Rennert
EXECUTIVE MANAGING EDITOR    Karyn Gullen Browne
EXECUTIVE EDITOR    Sean Dolan
COPY CHIEF    Philip Koslow
PICTURE EDITOR    Adrian G. Allen
ART DIRECTOR    Nora Wertz
MANUFACTURING DIRECTOR    Gerald Levine
SYSTEMS MANAGER    Lindsey Ottman
PRODUCTION COORDINATOR    Marie Claire Cebrián-Ume

**JUNIOR WORLD BIOGRAPHIES**

SENIOR EDITOR: Kathy Kuhtz

Staff for JOAN OF ARC

COPY EDITOR    David Carter
EDITORIAL ASSISTANT    Robert Kimball Green
SENIOR DESIGNER    Marjorie Zaum
PICTURE RESEARCHER    Sandy Jones

3  5  7  9  8  6  4  2

Library of Congress Cataloging-in-Publication Data
Christopher, Tracy.
Joan of Arc/Tracy Christopher
    p.  cm.—(Junior world biographies)
Includes biographical references and index.
Summary: A biography of the fifteenth-century peasant girl who led a French
army to victory against the English, witnessed the crowning of King Charles VII,
and was later burned at the stake for witchcraft.
ISBN 0-7910-1767-2
ISBN 0-7910-1986-1 (pbk.)
1. Joan, of Arc, Saint 1412–1431—Juvenile literature.  2. Christian Saints—
France—Biography—Juvenile literature.  3. France—History—Charles VII,
1422–1461—Juvenile literature. [1. Joan, of Arc, Saint, 1422–1431. 2. Saints.
3. France—History—Charles VII, 1422–1461.] I. Title. II. Series.
DC103.5.C47 1993                                                    92-20044
944'.026'092—dc20                                                   CIP
[B]                                                                 AC

# Contents

*Joan of Arc, saint and national heroine of France, as portrayed by the French artist Jean-Auguste-Dominique Ingres (1780–1867).*

# 1

# To Save France

---

The rulers of England and France had long quarreled over which country had the right to rule the other. For hundreds of years the ruling families of the two countries had been connected by marriages and tangled lines of descent and inheritance. In 1066, the Normans of France, led by Duke William, a cousin of the English king Edward, conquered England. Duke William became King William I of England. Although the victorious Normans had come from Normandy, a *duchy* (a territory ruled by a duke or duchess), in the northwestern part of France, they soon began to think of themselves as English.

By the early 14th century, with the Normans still on the throne of England, fighting between the French and English kingdoms had started again. This time the fight was over who should control France. For almost a century England and France fought each other in a series of battles that became known as the Hundred Years War.

By the early 15th century, the English held most of northern France, including the capital city of Paris. In 1420, after the Burgundians and the English took Troyes, a city on the Seine River, King Charles VI of France was forced to sign the Treaty of Troyes. (The Burgundians, Frenchmen who lived in the duchy of Burgundy, a region that extended beyond the northeastern part of France into most of what are today Belgium and the Netherlands, were ruled by Philip, the duke of Burgundy. They sided with the English.) Historians believe that King Charles VI was actually insane when he agreed to the terms of the Treaty of Troyes, and he was later called Charles the Foolish.

By signing the treaty, Charles VI practically gave France to England. He agreed to allow the English king Henry V to take the title of *regent* and heir to the throne of France. (A regent is someone who rules during the absence or disability of the king.) King Henry V, in turn, agreed to marry Charles's youngest daughter, Catherine. Finally, and most important, both kings formally banned the *dauphin*, the oldest son of the king of France, from all future negotiations and treaties. Furthermore, the Treaty of Troyes kept the dauphin, whose name was also Charles, from ever becoming king of France.

King Henry V married Catherine in 1420. In 1422, they had a son, Henry VI of England. In the same year, King Charles VI and King Henry V both died. Their sons now became rivals for the throne of France. At the time, Charles VII was 19 years old, and Henry VI was only 9 months old. However, the English quickly appointed baby Henry's uncle, the duke of Bedford, as regent and gave him power to rule France. Another uncle, the duke of Gloucester, became protector of England until Henry VI would be old enough to govern.

The duke of Bedford was a powerful man and commanded an enormous army. He also had the support of the dauphin's cousin—and enemy—Philip, the duke of Burgundy.

The dauphin, who was a physically small and frail young man, had no desire to fight or to involve himself in the war with England, even if it meant losing his own kingdom. Moreover, his father, King Charles VI, and mother, Queen Isabeau, had officially *disinherited* him and had planted serious doubts in his mind as to who his real father was.

The dauphin faced two very powerful enemies—the duke of Bedford and the duke of Burgundy—who had tremendous resources in money, land, and men. The dauphin had practically no money and had been driven into the southwestern portion of France, into lands along the Loire River. The Loire separated the English and French sections of France. Many of the people in the towns and cities that had once been part of the French kingdom had abandoned the dauphin and had sworn allegiance to either the duke of Burgundy or the duke of Bedford.

A small number of experienced French military commanders wanted the dauphin to back up his claim to the throne, with force if necessary. Unfortunately, Charles VII refused to launch a major attack against the English or against his cousin, Duke Philip. Two advisers, Georges de la Tremoille and Regnault de Chartres, persuaded Charles to remain at home in Chinon, where he enjoyed his life at the royal *court*, while the English and Burgundians chipped away his kingdom, piece by piece.

At a time when the situation looked hopeless for the dauphin and the French, rumors began to circulate across the land. During the Middle Ages people believed in legends, stories that were handed down through the ages and that many people thought were true even though they could not prove them to be. People recalled a prediction that the legendary *wizard* Merlin had once supposedly made. He had said that France would one day be ruined by a woman of loose morals from a foreign land, but then saved by a maid from Lorraine (a farming duchy in the north of France).

The first part of Merlin's *prophecy* had been fulfilled. People believed that the woman from a foreign land was surely Queen Isabeau, the dauphin's mother, who was from Bavaria (today a region in southeastern Germany). Queen Isabeau seemed unashamed of her frequent affairs with her husband's attendants, called *courtiers*, and turned her back on the rightful heir of France, her son Charles VII.

But who could be the maid from Lorraine who would fulfill the second part of Merlin's prophecy? People would soon come to believe that Joan of Arc, a peasant born in the village of Domremy in Lorraine, was the maid sent by God to save France.

*Twelve-year-old Joan listens to the voices of Saint Michael, Saint Catherine, and Saint Margaret. The voices told Joan that she would end the siege of Orleans and lead the dauphin to his coronation in Rheims.*

# 2

# Joan's Childhood and Setting Out

There is no written record of what Joan of Arc actually looked like. Historians would not know much about her at all if she had not been involved in two of the most important trials of the Middle Ages. In the first trial, she was condemned to death as a *heretic* for refusing to obey the teachings of the Catholic church. This was a serious offense in France at the time.

In the second trial, which took place nearly 20 years after her death, authorities questioned 115 witnesses to determine if Joan had been falsely accused. Many pages of testimony paint a vivid picture of her childhood and adult life, including statements from members of the French court who tell of her deeds as one of Charles VII's greatest captains.

Joan was born in the village of Domremy in 1412. Her father, Jacques Darc (later mistakenly written "D'arc," which in English means "of Arc"), was a peasant but owned a house and a little land. Domremy was located in territory partially controlled by the duke of Burgundy.

Young Joan's life was hard. Peasant children did not go to school. As soon as she was old enough, Joan worked with her sister and three brothers on the family farm. She learned to spin wool and to sew. She also herded the family's cattle and sheep.

Joan's parents raised her to be a pious Catholic. Her mother taught her the Paternoster (the Lord's Prayer) and other prayers. People of the village remembered that Joan went often to church and to confession. They also said that she was kind to the poor, to the sick, and to children.

Joan was a lot like other peasant girls of Domremy until she was 12 years old. One day, she stopped to rest under a large tree. Suddenly she saw a great light and began to hear voices. She later discovered that the voices speaking to her were those of Saint Michael, Saint Catherine, and Saint Margaret. At her 1431 trial, Joan said:

> When I was 12, I had a voice from God to help me to govern myself. The first time, I was terrified. The voice came to me about noon: it was summer, and I was in my father's garden. I heard the voice on my right hand, towards the church. There was a great light all about. . . . I vowed then to keep my virginity for as long as it should please God. . . . I saw [the great light] many times before I knew that it was St. Michael. . . . He told me that St. Catherine and St. Margaret would come to me, and that I must follow their advice. He told me

*Joan grew up in this house (left) in Domremy and was baptized in the church next door. Joan, whose parents were peasants, worked with her sister and three brothers on the family farm.*

the pitiful state of the kingdom of France. Twice and thrice a week the voice told me that I must depart and go into France [the country still controlled by the dauphin, Charles]. . . . And the voice said that I would raise the siege before Orleans. And it told me to go to Vaucouleurs, to Robert de

18

Baudricourt, captain of the town, who would give me men to go with me. . . . And I answered the voice that I was a poor girl who knew nothing of riding and warfare.

Joan did not tell anyone in the village that she had heard voices. At first, Joan doubted that she had the skills to do what the voices commanded. For four years Joan continued to live her life and to work on the farm as she had always done. People in the village remembered that she seemed a little more serious and devout: in addition to going to church, she retreated to the woods to pray at a small shrine.

The voices came to her more frequently. In May 1428, when she was 16, Joan decided to make the journey to Vaucouleurs: "I went to my uncle's and there I stayed about eight days. And I told my uncle that I must go to the town of Vaucouleurs and my uncle took me there." She kept her plans to herself because she was afraid that no one would believe her story.

When she arrived at Vaucouleurs, she asked to meet with Robert de Baudricourt, the captain of the town. At first he refused to see her because she was a peasant girl who had seemingly strange ideas.

When Joan finally met Robert de Baudricourt, she was honest and direct: "It is the will of my Lord that the Dauphin be made king and have the kingdom in his command. In spite of my enemies he will be king. I myself shall conduct him to his crowning."

"Who is your Lord?" Baudricourt asked.

"The King of Heaven," Joan replied.

Baudricourt laughed. He did not believe her. He recommended that she be sent home to her father and punished. He absolutely refused to help her.

Joan went home deeply discouraged. She decided to give up her plan and to ignore the voices. But the voices would not let her alone. They kept urging her to return to Vaucouleurs. Matters were getting worse for the French. In the fall of 1428, word spread that the Burgundian army was about to attack Domremy. All the people in Domremy had to flee to a nearby walled town for protection.

In October 1428, the English laid siege to Orleans. Orleans was one of the few large and wealthy cities remaining loyal to the French dauphin, Charles. The French also valued Orleans as a military stronghold; the city had flourished on the banks of the Loire River as a trade city and commanded one of the only bridges across the river. If Orleans fell, the English could continue south and conquer other lands in Charles VII's dwindling kingdom.

When news reached Domremy of the siege at Orleans, the people in Joan's village feared that the English would succeed this time and would conquer all of France. England and Burgundy would simply divide the kingdom between them, and Domremy would fall under the rule of the hated Burgundians.

The voices Joan heard became more and more insistent: she must return to Vaucouleurs and convince Robert de Baudricourt to send her to the dauphin. In January 1429, at the age of 17, Joan left secretly for Vaucouleurs. She did not tell her family or friends that she was leaving, although she doubted that she would ever see anyone in her village again.

Joan was taken in by a wheelwright (a person who makes and repairs wheels), Henri le Royer, and his wife, Catherine. Joan stayed with them for three weeks before Baudricourt agreed to meet with her again. During this time, Joan impressed the whole town by her pious ways. She went to church and to confession, and she showed kindness to the poor and sick. She also met Jean de Metz and Bertrand de Poulengy, two knights who listened enthusiastically to her story and offered to accompany her to see the dauphin.

Jean de Metz and Bertrand de Poulengy encouraged Baudricourt to speak with Joan. Then a messenger, sent by the dauphin, arrived at Vaucouleurs. Apparently the talk about the young woman who wanted to save France had reached the dauphin, and he wanted to hear Joan's story himself.

Baudricourt did not believe in help sent from heaven in the form of a 17-year-old girl, but he sent for Joan anyway. He had to give his permission for her to travel to the town of Chinon, where the dauphin lived in a castle with his royal court. Chinon was about a 10-day ride by horse from Vaucouleurs. Jean de Metz and Bertrand de Poulengy decided to escort Joan and to pay her expenses.

By this time Joan was very popular with the townspeople of Vaucouleurs. A cousin and his friend had saved enough money to buy her a horse. Because it would be safer to travel dressed as a young man, Joan exchanged her red peasant's dress for the clothes that a page (a boy training to be a knight) at the French court would wear: a black doublet, which is a close-fitting jacket, a short, dark gray tunic, and a black cap. Several ladies at Vaucouleurs made her the outfit as a gift. Others brought her high boots and spurs.

Finally even Robert de Baudricourt joined in the enthusiastic send-off. He gave Joan a sword and embraced her when she left on February 23, 1429. Just to make sure that she was God's agent and not the Devil's, he sent a priest to drive out any evil spirits that might be within her.

After 12 days of riding safely through enemy territory, Joan reached Chinon on March 6. Later, a member of the French court described the first meeting between Joan and the dauphin in the castle at Chinon. The future king had tried to remain anonymous to test Joan's powers: "When the king knew she was coming, he withdrew apart from the others. Joan, however, knew him at once and made him a reverence and spoke to him for some time." To this day, no one knows exactly what Joan said to Charles. Perhaps she proved to him that he was the rightful heir to the throne and convinced him with the answers to his questions. After his meeting with Joan, Charles suddenly seemed very happy and ready to put his trust in her.

Everyone in France prayed for a miracle. Marguerite la Touroulde, a member of the royal court, later described the effect of Joan's arrival at Charles's castle:

> At that time, there was in his kingdom and in those parts obedient to the king such calamity and such

poverty that it was pitiful, and indeed those true to their allegiance to the king were in despair. . . . And the city of Orleans was besieged by the English and there was no means of going to its aid. And it was in the midst of this calamity that Joan came, and, I believe it firmly, she came from God and was sent to raise up the king and the people still within his allegiance, for at that time there was no hope but in God.

Many people at the French court believed that Joan was telling the truth about the voices she heard. They thought that God had sent her to help them. The dauphin, however, wanted as much proof of this as possible. He sent Joan south to the city of Poitiers to be investigated and tested by the learned men of the Church.

The investigation began in March 1429 and lasted for six weeks. At only one point during the questioning did Joan lose her patience. The churchmen asked for clear signs that she was from God. "I have not come to Poitiers to make signs,"

*In this 15th-century German tapestry, Joan arrives at Chinon and is greeted by Charles VII. Before placing his trust in Joan, Charles sent her to Poitiers to be tested by the learned men of the Catholic church.*

she exclaimed. "Take me to Orleans and I will show you the signs for which I have been sent."

Joan gave details about the "signs" her voices had outlined. She promised to do three things. She promised to end the siege of Orleans, to see the dauphin crowned at Rheims, and to drive the English out of France. These things seemed impossible. The English were firmly established at Orleans. The city of Rheims and all the lands around it were occupied by the English. The French would have to win many difficult battles, and they did not have enough men, supplies, or money.

Nevertheless, the Poitiers scholars could find no reason to disbelieve Joan. The longer they observed her daily life, the harder it was to be suspicious of this simple peasant girl. In her personal habits, Joan was well mannered, pious, serious, and moderate. She showed great compassion for the city's people in need and a special love for its children. The people in Poitiers grew to love her.

At last, in mid-April, the churchmen made their decision. They declared that Joan was "a good Christian and Catholic." They recommended that the dauphin rely on her.

Charles lost no time after Joan's return trip from Poitiers. He sent Joan north to Tours, where his knights prepared her equipment for battle. She had a standard (flag) made, on which was an image of Christ sitting in judgment, with two angels beside him holding the royal flower, the fleur-de-lis (lily).

While Joan was at Tours, the voices told her that a sword had been buried behind the altar of Saint Catherine's Church at Fierbois. Joan sent a messenger to the town to ask the priests to look for the sword. Extremely surprised, the priests discovered a sword with five crosses on its hilt, just as Joan had predicted. The sword looked too old to use in battle, but when it was polished, the rust disappeared quickly.

When Joan had all of her equipment ready, including her standard and her sword, she was ready to meet the troops at the city of Blois. Joan left for the army's general headquarters on April 22, 1429. Priests singing hymns marched at the head of the great army as it moved from Blois toward Orleans.

*The maid from Domremy leads the French troops at the battle of Orleans in May 1429. The duke of Alencon was amazed by Joan's ability to fight and to find the best places for artillery, even though she had no military training.*

# 3

# The Sudden Victory

During the Middle Ages, people who lived in important cities, such as Orleans, built high stone walls around their cities to protect them from enemy attack. Nearby farmers had brought animals, food, and other belongings within the protective walls of Orleans, and the townspeople found it a safe haven.

However, the English had built 10 bastions, or guard towers, outside the city walls at strategic places so that they could prevent shipments of food from reaching the townspeople. Whenever French soldiers or citizens were within firing range, the English shot arrows at them and launched enormous stones from catapults.

By laying siege to Orleans, the English hoped to starve the citizens, forcing them to surrender. By the time Joan arrived in April 1429, the fighting had already been going on for seven months; sieges during the Middle Ages often lasted for many months or even years.

Joan rode with the duke of Alencon at the head of 6,000 troops, loaded supply wagons, and 400 cattle, to relieve the soldiers who fought against the English. Joan and the others counted on the support of 3,000 soldiers already within the walls of Orleans. The French had also armed 5,000 of the 30,000 residents of the city. They had been attacking the English bastions in small groups since October. But the seven months of fighting without a decisive victory had left the defenders of Orleans exhausted and discouraged.

From Blois, the French army traveled about 34 miles to reach Orleans. Both cities were located on the north bank of the Loire River. The quickest route to Orleans was to the north, but to enter Orleans from that direction meant that the French army would have to lead the cattle and supply wagons through territory that was heavily guarded by the English.

Instead, the captains decided to go farther north, to Checy, five miles from Orleans. Using

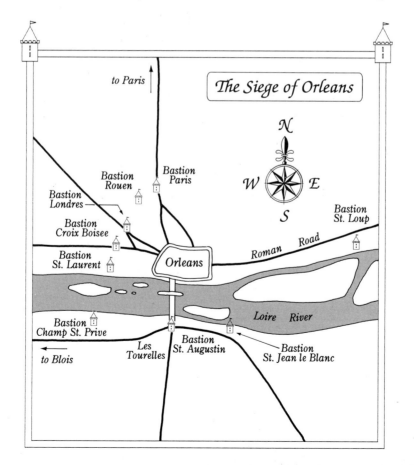

barges, they would then float the supplies down the Loire to Orleans. The army would enter the city through the Burgundy Gate, one of the openings in the wall protecting the city.

This route appeared to be the best for two reasons. First, the nearest English bastion, St. Loup, was three miles from the river, so the boats might pass by it unnoticed. Second, the old Roman road leading to the Burgundy Gate was controlled by Philip, the duke of Burgundy. For years Philip had been the sworn enemy of his cousin the dauphin, but he had become angry with the English after they had refused to give him the city of Orleans to govern. The French captains hoped the duke would let them pass unharmed—and he eventually did.

The captains did not consult Joan when they decided to take the army to Checy. Because she had no military training, she had not been put in charge of the campaign. When they reached the south bank of the Loire, Joan realized that they would waste valuable time crossing the river to get to Orleans. She was furious at the delay and at the captains for leaving her out of their plan. To make matters worse, a strong wind blew in the wrong direction, making the trip with the supply boats impossible.

Joan went to a nearby field to pray for advice. Suddenly the wind shifted. Everyone was amazed at the change. They thought that God had answered Joan's prayer. Joan and a small number of troops crossed the Loire with the supply boats and entered Orleans on Friday, April 29, 1429. The rest of the army made the two-day march back to Blois to seek reinforcements.

The citizens of Orleans treated Joan like a legendary heroine when she brought food to the starving city. Because she—a woman—wore armor she was also a curiosity. Everyone wanted to touch Joan's armor, horse, and standard as she rode through the streets of Orleans.

The next day, and the day after that, Joan stood on the bridge and faced the English, commanding them to retreat and leave France, in the name of the dauphin, Charles, and of the King of Heaven. The English had a perfect opportunity to shoot or capture Joan while she stood on the bridge, but they only shouted insults at her. They did not take her orders seriously.

The English had two other opportunities to capture or harm Joan. On May 1, Joan rode from the city with the count of Dunois, the French commander at Orleans. The count was on his way to Blois to meet the advancing army of French reinforcements. The English could have captured both Joan and one of the most important leaders of the French army, but they did not. Then on May 4, Joan left Orleans with 500 men to meet the troops arriving from Blois. Historians cannot explain why the English allowed all 6,000 troops to enter the city unopposed. It was as if something had paralyzed them.

On May 4, Joan learned that English reinforcements under the leadership of Sir John Fastolf were marching toward Orleans. It was time to act. Joan took part in a skirmish outside the Burgundy

Gate early in the morning on Thursday, May 5. The French forces burned and demolished the small bastion of St. Loup; 114 English soldiers died and 40 were taken prisoner.

The duke of Alencon said later how surprised he was that Joan seemed such an expert in war. She could array armies for battle and find the best places for artillery. Yet she had never had any military training. The duke of Alencon said, "And at that all marvelled, that she could act in so prudent and well-advised a fashion in the matter of war as might a captain of twenty or thirty years' experience have done."

On Friday, May 6, against the wishes of Raoul de Gaucourt, one of the dauphin's most influential counselors, Joan and another captain fought for and then took the smaller bastion of St. Jean le Blanc. They then led an all-day assault on the much larger bastion, St. Augustin. Eventually the English had to retreat to the still bigger bastion of Les Tourelles. French forces spent the night guarding their reconquered territory.

Les Tourelles blocked the only bridge over the Loire. It was the strongest of all the English defenses. The French captains thought that their men were too tired to fight the next day. They did not want to attack, but Joan was determined to force the English to retreat. She decided to lead the attack even though her voices told her that she would be wounded in the battle.

Warfare during the Middle Ages was as brutal as today, only slower. A soldier often fought with a sword, a lance, or a bow and arrows. The storming of a bastion involved considerable hand-to-hand combat. Soldiers used scaling ladders, which they laid against the walls of a bastion, and then they climbed to the top to fight it out there. A few hours of this kind of combat were all most soldiers could endure.

The fighting at Les Tourelles lasted from 7:00 in the morning until 8:00 at night. At noon, an arrow pierced Joan's left shoulder. It was a serious wound, six inches deep; soldiers wanted to place a charm on the wound to heal it, but Joan did not believe in superstitious magic. She had the wound treated with olive oil and lard, a common medical remedy at the time.

At the end of the day, it had become too dark for the troops to see to fight, and the French captains had lost hope of winning the battle. They sounded the retreat. Joan heard the sound from a nearby vineyard where she was praying. She returned to the battle and urged the captains to make one last charge.

Holding her standard high, she rallied the men and was the first to place a scaling ladder against the bridge. The count of Dunois later recalled the scene: "The moment she was there the English trembled and were terrified. And the king's soldiers regained courage and began to go up, charging against the [bastion] without meeting the least resistance."

In their flight from Les Tourelles, the English ran over the bridge. Suddenly, the bridge

*The young heroine pulls an arrow from her shoulder after she is wounded by the English during the Battle of Les Tourelles. After treating her wound and praying, Joan returned to the battle to lead the troops in one last charge.*

collapsed. All of the 600 Englishmen defending the bastion were killed, drowned, or taken prisoner. Joan wept at the death of so many.

On Sunday, May 8, the English ended their siege. They came out of their bastions, where they had been safe, and prepared to meet the French in open battle in a nearby field.

Sundays, however, were considered days of truce. On Sunday, the Lord's day, a day of rest and worship, it was considered sinful to attack an enemy, but it was totally righteous to defend oneself if attacked.

For several hours, the English and French armies confronted each other. Joan refused to let the French attack; instead, she had her confessor, Jean Pasquerel, celebrate two masses, with the French soldiers serving as his congregation.

Finally the English marched away, without fighting, and headed toward the town of Meung. They lost cannon, crossbows, and other artillery during their retreat.

On that day, May 8, the city of Orleans celebrated its liberation from the English. In fact, even today Orleans commemorates its freedom every May 8 in the same way: the citizens participate in candle-lit processions to all the churches throughout the city.

The people of Orleans and the army captains also honored Joan's heroism. Jean Pasquerel later recalled: "It was said to her: Never have been seen such things as you have been seen to do; in no book are to be read of deeds like them."

The English, of course, were not pleased with the outcome at Orleans. They had been badly shaken by Joan's sudden victory. They feared and resented Joan for her ability to inspire French soldiers to fight.

The duke of Bedford—the regent of France—believed that Joan was a *witch*. In the letter he wrote to England to tell of his losses, he described Joan as "a disciple and limb of the Fiend." On hearing of Joan's victories, many Englishmen who had been drafted to fight in France refused to go.

Surprisingly, the dauphin did not seem overjoyed at the news of Joan's victories, although he was certainly not angry. In fact, he rewarded Joan with a generous sum of money. He also invited her to stay at his castle. However, when he wrote a proclamation about the great victory, he mentioned Joan's name only at the end. He gave most of the credit to the armies and to their commanders. And when the heroic young woman asked to lead Charles to the city of Rheims to be crowned king, he refused to go. Wavering, Charles asked her to be patient.

*Joan of Arc attends the coronation of Charles VII in Rheims Cathedral on July 17, 1429. The coronation was the second of the three tasks Joan's voices had commanded her to achieve.*

# 4
# A True King and a Declared Heretic

After the victory at Orleans, Joan rejoined the dauphin and his court on May 10, 1429. She urged Charles to take advantage of the English defeat at Orleans. He could now travel north to the city of Rheims, where French kings were crowned.

Charles wasted a month of valuable time making objections. But on May 23, Charles consulted his military and political council. The council decided that the army should prepare the way to Rheims and that Charles should follow it.

One of the council members said later: "And, although the king had no money to pay his army, all the knights, esquires, men of war, and of the commonality [common people] did not refuse to go with and serve him for that journey in the Maid's company, saying that wheresoever she went, they would go."

Throughout the week of June 10, the French army defeated the English and recovered the cities of Jargeau, Meung, Beaugency, and Patay. More than 5,000 English soldiers were killed or taken prisoner, and the French captured two prominent English commanders, the earl of Suffolk and Lord Talbot.

The dauphin met with very little resistance as he passed through Burgundian territory that had been recovered for France. The cities of Auxerre, Troyes, and Chalons declared themselves loyal to Charles as he passed through them. And when Charles entered Rheims on July 16, 1429, people cried "Noel! Noel!" (the ancient way of saying, "Long live the king!").

The French believed that for a king to be properly crowned, the ceremony had to take place in Rheims. Clovis, the first Christian king of France, had been crowned there by Saint Remy in 496. One legend is that during this ceremony, God sent a white dove to bring the Sainte Ampoule (Holy Vial) to Saint Remy. The Sainte Ampoule was a small bottle made of crystal. It was about an inch long and was capped by a red silk stopper. The Sainte Ampoule contained oil that was believed to have been blessed by God. By annointing the king—by putting a small amount of this oil on the king's forehead—his whole being became sacred. It was believed, then, that his power to command came directly from God. As God's servant and representative on earth, the king promised to uphold God's law and to treat his subjects justly and mercifully, just as God would do. A king was, therefore, expected to act for the good of his people.

The Sainte Ampoule was the sacred possession of the cathedral at Rheims. For 13 centuries, church officials had not allowed anyone to take it from the city. Consequently, every French king had to travel to Rheims for his *coronation.*

On July 17, 1429, almost 1,000 years after the first ceremony, the Sainte Ampoule was opened once again, and a golden pin was stuck into the vial to extract a small portion of its contents.

Wearing her armor and carrying her standard, Joan stood behind the dauphin as he kneeled. She watched as the archbishop of Rheims consecrated, or blessed, Charles VII as the true king of France.

The second of the three tasks Joan's voices had commanded her to perform had been accomplished. She had every reason to believe that God had given Charles VII the power to rule France and to drive the English out of the country forever.

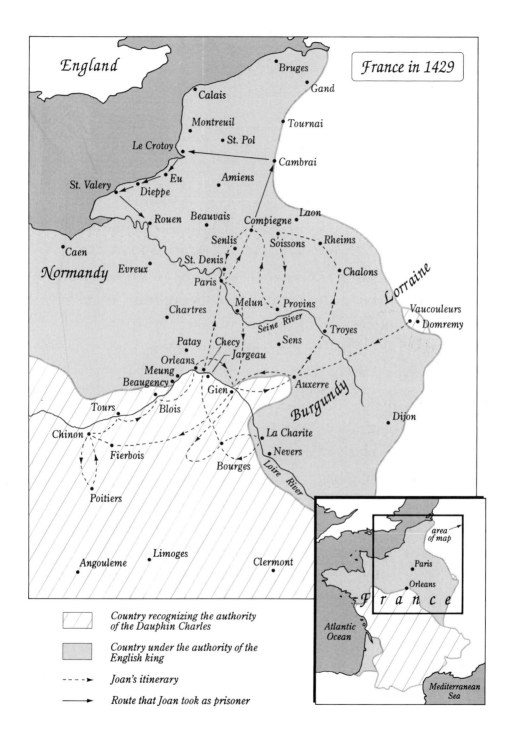

England

France in 1429

Bruges

Gand

Calais

Montreuil

St. Pol

Tournai

Le Crotoy

Cambrai

St. Valery

Eu

Amiens

Dieppe

Rouen

Beauvais

Laon

Compiegne

Caen

Evreux

Senlis

Soissons

Rheims

Normandy

St. Denis

Chalons

Lorraine

Paris

Vaucouleurs

Chartres

Melun

Provins

Domremy

Seine River

Troyes

Patay

Checy

Sens

Orleans

Jargeau

Auxerre

Meung

Beaugency

Gien

Burgundy

Tours

Blois

Dijon

Chinon

La Charite

Fierbois

Nevers

Bourges

Loire River

Poitiers

Angouleme

Limoges

Clermont

area
of map

Atlantic
Ocean

Paris

Orleans

France

Mediterranean
Sea

Country recognizing the authority
of the Dauphin Charles

Country under the authority of the
English king

- - - ▸   Joan's itinerary

⟶   Route that Joan took as prisoner

Once the news about Charles's coronation had spread across the land, the cities of Soissons, Laon, Compiegne, Beauvais, Senlis, and St. Denis sent word that they, too, were ready to resist the English. The English reacted to this loss of power by sending the boy king Henry VI to France. On April 23, 1430, eight-year-old Henry VI came to Rouen to live.

After the ceremony at Rheims, Joan urged Charles to travel farther north to Paris, which was still controlled by the English. After winning so many victories, Joan believed it was wise to push ahead before the English could recover.

But the French lost four precious days while Charles, under the influence of counselors secretly allied to the duke of Burgundy, negotiated a treaty with the English and Burgundians. During that time, the duke of Bedford brought 3,500 English troops to reinforce the English army in Paris.

Rather than head north and attack Paris, Charles went south, where he could be safe in territory that he already controlled. He even signed treaties allowing Burgundy to remain independent. He also returned to Duke Philip many of the cities that had recently come over to Charles's side.

The English negotiated with Charles in order to stall the French army from advancing. They also tried to dishonor Joan in the eyes of the French. Their negotiators implied that the French king depended on a woman who was rumored to be a witch.

Charles signed another treaty with the English on August 21, 1429. This agreement was supposed to remain in effect until April 16, 1430. The French promised not to invade Normandy, which was occupied by the English. The treaty also appointed the duke of Bedford to the post of governor of Paris.

Angered and disappointed about these treaties, Joan continued to urge Charles to attack Paris, which was exempt from the cease-fire. On September 8, 1429, Charles finally allowed Joan and the duke of Alencon to assemble an army to march on Paris. Two months had passed since the king's coronation at Rheims. The English had used the time well to build stronger fortifications around the city.

Joan and the duke of Alencon had to raise the army by themselves. Charles refused to help them, and his lack of support confused Joan. He even ordered some of his soldiers to burn a bridge that provided access to Paris from the south. Then, to make matters worse, on September 21, 1429, Charles disbanded the knights that had been with Joan since the siege of Orleans. He ordered them to go to various towns in the north of France, and Joan was not allowed to join them.

Joan never openly criticized the king. Instead, she blamed his counselors for having advised him badly. Her voices told her that her time was running out and that she would be captured before St. John's Day (June 24) of the next year. Charles, however, seemed absolutely unwilling to continue fighting. Near despair after ordering a retreat, Joan decided to leave her armor as an offering before the image of Mary, mother of Jesus, in the Abbey of St. Denis.

Charles's desire to frustrate Joan became increasingly clear. From September 1429 to April 1430, he kept her from becoming involved in any more fighting, while he negotiated with the English. Charles rewarded Joan with money and invited her to stay at several of his castles. He also raised her family to the rank of nobility and excused her native village of Domremy from paying any more royal taxes. Meanwhile another 2,000 English troops, led by the duke of Bedford, arrived in Paris.

In April 1430, Joan set out without the king's permission to relieve Compiegne. On the way there, she stopped at the city of Melun to spend Holy Week, the week before Easter during which the last days of Christ's life are honored.

Joan observed all the holy days of the Catholic church. In fact, she practiced her religion faithfully even under the most difficult conditions. She asked that mass be held every morning, even before a battle. She did not allow French soldiers to swear or gamble, and she urged them to go to confession so that they would not die with their sins unpardoned.

On May 23, 1430, Joan and her troops attacked the English who were besieging Compiegne. The battle did not go well; the French were forced to retreat into the walled city. Joan and a small group of soldiers brought up the rear to protect the retreating army. The English managed to cut them off and to surround them. The mayor of Compiegne left the drawbridge down as long as he dared but raised it when the English seemed about to overtake the town. More than 400 French soldiers died that day in the battle.

John of Luxembourg, a nobleman in the service of Duke Philip, captured Joan. When Duke Philip found out that Joan had been captured, he asked for 10,000 francs in ransom money. The English quickly agreed to accept the ransom. Charles, however, did not offer to pay the ransom, perhaps because he did not have enough money. His failure to act to obtain Joan's release puzzles historians even today.

After they had gotten Joan, the English had no intention of releasing her. John of Luxembourg was appointed to guard her in his castle of Beaurevoir. From May to December 1430, Joan was locked up in a tower 70 feet high and was constantly watched by three women—John's wife, his mother-in-law, and his stepdaughter.

Then, one morning, Joan was found unconscious on the rocks below the tower. She had tried to escape by jumping from the roof. She remained unconscious for two days but miraculously had not suffered any broken bones.

The English took no more chances with Joan after her attempt to escape. They transferred her to a gloomy cell in a castle in Rouen. At that time, Rouen was the most pro-English city in all of France. The English had governed Rouen for 10 years, and Henry VI of England lived there in order

*Joan was imprisoned in this castle in Rouen, France, in 1431.*

to gather up enough force to make his claim to the throne of France.

English officials had persuaded the Catholic church to try Joan in court as a heretic. They wanted to prove that her power did not really come from God, and they accused her of being a witch. These two charges—of being a heretic and a witch—were among the most severe crimes a person could be accused of during the Middle Ages.

The English wanted to disgrace Joan so that neither the French nor the English soldiers would respect her. They also hoped that by discrediting her, they would foil Charles's attempt to regain his kingdom.

*While Joan, in chains, lies in prison, Bishop Cauchon questions her about the voices she heard, trying to prove that she was an agent of the Devil. After Joan's trial, the bishop ordered the scribes to alter her testimony.*

# 5

# The Maid's Fate

Joan's trial lasted five months, from January 9 to May 30, 1431. It was obvious from the beginning, however, that the English intended to treat the young woman from Domremy as a political prisoner with no rights. Usually when a woman was accused of heresy, she was locked up in the archbishop's prison and guarded by women. The cells there were fairly comfortable, and the prisoner was allowed to hear mass daily and to move freely around the grounds of the prison.

But Joan was imprisoned in the dungeon of the castle at Rouen, and English soldiers guarded her. She repeatedly complained about being mistreated by them. She was locked in chains, was not allowed to hear mass, and was deprived of confession along with the other rites of her religion.

It became clear to most of the French that the English meant to imprison Joan for the rest of her life or, even worse, to execute her. Perhaps the English worried that killing her while people still believed in her might make her a *martyr*, and her power would grow even greater.

The English paid Pierre Cauchon, a French bishop who was loyal to them, to try Joan. Bishop Cauchon first had to find grounds to accuse Joan of being a witch.

On January 9, he began to question Joan about the voices she heard, implying that they came from the Devil. Bishop Cauchon also intended to prove that Joan was an impure and cruel woman because she had been a soldier.

Joan managed to avoid being caught in the many legalistic traps the bishop set for her. One of the trickiest questions she was asked was: "Do you know if you are in God's grace?" She knew that if she answered yes, she would be claiming to know something only God knew. Yet if she answered no, she could be accused of being an agent of the Devil. Joan avoided both dangers. "If I am not," she answered, "may God bring me to it; if I am, may God keep me in it." Many people at the trial felt that not even the clever churchmen who questioned her could have answered so well.

It was clear to everyone present that Joan's trial was not being conducted according to the usual rules. Bishop Cauchon refused to allow her to have a lawyer or anyone to speak on her behalf. He also refused Joan's request to plead her case before the pope, the head of the Catholic church. Bishop Cauchon was afraid that the pope might believe in Joan's innocence and then might forbid the trial to continue.

Secretly, Bishop Cauchon ordered the *scribes*, the men writing down Joan's testimony, to alter what she had said. Joan's words were twisted into statements that eventually condemned her.

The bishop's main accusation was that Joan would not submit to the law of the *Church Militant* (the church on earth), but instead placed her loyalty in God alone. At this time, officials of the Catholic church claimed to receive power and inspiration directly from God in order to win souls. To obey the Catholic church and its officials also meant to love and obey God. Even the slightest refusal to submit in any way to the Church's authority was reason enough to convict a person of heresy.

The Church ordered Joan to deny that the voices she heard came from God. She had to agree to abandon her mission, to resume wearing women's clothes rather than those of a page, and to perform traditional women's duties.

Joan's resolve remained strong until May 24, 1430, when she was taken to Saint-Ouen, a cemetery outside of Rouen. Bishop Cauchon had a scaffold and stake built and warned Joan that she would be burned as a heretic unless she *recanted*, or took back her previous statements. Of all the ways to die, Joan feared death by fire the most. At the last moment, fear overwhelmed her, and she recanted.

Bishop Cauchon quickly read, and then had Joan sign, a short statement. It said that she renounced her voices, agreed to wear women's clothes, and consented to spend the rest of her life in prison praying for forgiveness for her sins. Later, in the official trial records, Bishop Cauchon illegally replaced the eight-line statement with a much longer one (one that Joan had never read or signed), which accused her of much more serious crimes.

Joan was not sent to the archbishop's prison, as was required by Church law, but instead was sent back to the castle at Rouen to spend the rest of her life in chains. Four days later, after she regained her faith and courage, Joan put on men's clothes again. The reason for this is not clear. Perhaps the bishop had ordered the guards to hide her women's clothing. Or perhaps she felt safer wearing men's clothing because she was being guarded by English soldiers.

Nevertheless, by putting on men's clothes Joan had disobeyed the Church's orders. Bishop Cauchon accused her of being a relapsed heretic, someone who had resumed her evil ways. He now had an excuse to execute Joan. He might have been planning her execution all along.

On May 28, 1430, when Joan was brought before Church officials, she said: "All that I have done these last few days I did for fear of the fire, and my revocation [recantation] was against the truth. I have never done anything against God and against the faith, whatever I may have been made to revoke."

Joan clearly believed that she was innocent of crime. In fact, when Bishop Cauchon consulted the 42 churchmen he had assembled, only 2 of them were willing to declare her guilty of heresy. Unfortunately, the majority of these churchmen were not powerful, and Bishop Cauchon ignored their advice.

The Church did not allow its officials to carry out a death sentence. After declaring Joan a relapsed heretic, the Church turned to the sheriff of Rouen, a public official, who would carry out the sentence. During the reading of the sentence on May 30, Joan's emotions overwhelmed her. She began to pray aloud, and with tears in her eyes and great passion in her voice, she called on God and all of the saints. She begged for forgiveness from the crowd that had gathered around the scaffold and asked them to pray for her. She promised, in turn, to forgive them.

Soon many in the crowd had also begun to cry, including some of the churchmen and the

English soldiers. When Joan asked for a crucifix, it was an English soldier who rushed to lash two sticks together and then handed the cross to her.

Joan took this makeshift cross and stuffed it into the front of the old dress that she had been given to wear. An unearthly calm came over Joan. Then, quietly and with dignity, she mounted the great pile of wood at the base of the scaffold.

Joan stood still as the executioner tied her to the pole. She had just one request. Would someone go into the church, get the crucifix, bind it to a long stick, and hold it close to her face so that she might have the comfort of looking at it during her last moments? One of the churchmen raced into the church to do as she had asked.

The pile of wood was ignited and the flames rose quickly. As the crowd approached as close to the fire as it dared, Joan, whose dress had been soaked in sulphur to help it catch fire more quickly, cried out: "Jesus, Jesus, Jesus." And then, only the spitting of the fire could be heard. Joan's execution was all over.

At that last moment the French people saw that Joan had given all she could, even her life, to free France from English control. She had never lost faith in her cause; even her death was a victory because the English were as greatly moved by Joan's piety and courage as the French. Instead of feeling triumphant, the English felt distressed. What had they done by sending to her death a girl who in her last moments could say, "I forgive you!" and even call on *them*, her executioners, to forgive *her*?

"We are all lost," said one Englishman. "We have burned a saint." From that time on, the proud self-confidence that had been the source of so many English victories in France gradually began to erode.

Within 25 years of Joan's death at the stake in Rouen, the French had almost completely driven the English from France and reduced their

*Joan, clutching a makeshift cross, is burned at the stake in the market square of Rouen on May 30, 1431. In her last moments, Joan said to the surrounding crowd, "I forgive you!" She also asked her executioners to forgive her.*

holdings to just two cities (Bordeaux and Calais). Joan's death also had a particular effect on Charles VII. He finally became the courageous king Joan had always believed he could be.

Charles VII became a serious, brave monarch, and he chose his advisers more carefully than he had in the past. Several of the knights he chose to advise him had been Joan's strongest supporters. The king, who had seemed so fearful and unpromising when Joan knew him, was later called Charles the Victorious and Charles the Well-Advised by many historians.

In February 1450, as soon as he had reconquered Rouen and had access to the records of Joan's trial, Charles VII ordered an investigation of the proceedings. On March 4, Guillaume Manchon, the notary, or clerk, at Joan's trial, explained how the trial records, which were written in Latin, had been falsified. He handed over his copy of the original proceedings, written in French, that showed the extent to which Joan had been falsely condemned.

Five years later, Charles persuaded the Church to conduct a second trial to clear Joan's name. One hundred and fifteen witnesses testified during the second trial—Joan's friends and family from Domremy, participants in the original trial at Rouen, and several of Joan's closest companions in battle were heard.

This time the churchmen who conducted the retrial were honest. Finally, on July 7, 1456, the court declared that the original trial and sentence had included trickery and contradiction, and that serious errors of fact and of law had been made. In a symbolic act, the judges went to Rouen's Old Market Square, where Joan had been burned at the stake, and ripped up a copy of the original conviction and sentence. Pope Calixtus III declared Joan's name forever cleansed of all charges against it. And almost 500 years later, in 1920, the Catholic church *canonized* Joan—they made her a saint. Her feast day is May 30.

The attraction and power of Joan's story have grown with the passing of time. She has become a symbol for French nationalism and Catholicism. For example, when the Germans, under the dictatorship of Adolf Hitler, invaded France in 1940 during World War II, General Charles de Gaulle spoke of Joan's courage to rally French soldiers and civilians against their German foe.

Joan of Arc has been especially admired by people who have felt called to do tasks that are difficult or extremely dangerous. In her brief but valiant life they find the help they need to remain true, through whatever hardship or peril that comes their way, to the voice they hear within themselves.

# Further Reading

*Other Biographies of Joan of Arc*

Boutet De Monvel, Maurice. *Joan of Arc.* New York: Viking, 1980.

Johnston, Johanna. *Joan of Arc.* New York: Doubleday, 1961.

Nottridge, Harold. *Joan of Arc.* New York: Watts, 1988.

Sackville-West, V. *Saint Joan of Arc.* New York: Stackpole & Sons, 1938.

Storr, Catherine. *Joan of Arc.* Milwaukee, WI: Raintree, 1985.

# Chronology

| | |
|---|---|
| **1412** | Joan of Arc is born in Domremy, France. |
| **1420** | England and France sign the Treaty of Troyes. |
| **1424** | Joan first hears voices. |
| **May 1428** | Travels to the town of Vaucouleurs but fails to get the backing of Robert de Baudricourt for her mission to see the dauphin. |
| **Oct. 1428** | The siege of Orleans begins. |

| | |
|---|---|
| Jan. 1429 | Joan convinces Robert de Baudricourt that she must see the dauphin. |
| March 1429 | Meets the dauphin; is sent to Poitiers to be investigated by officials of the Roman Catholic church; gains the approval of churchmen at Poitiers. |
| Apr. 29, 1429 | Joan enters Orleans. |
| May 8, 1429 | Siege of Orleans is raised; the English troops retreat north of the Loire River. |
| July 17, 1429 | Charles VII is crowned at Rheims. |
| August 1429 | Charles VII signs a truce with Philip, the duke of Burgundy. |
| Sept. 1429 | French forces fail to take Paris; Joan of Arc leaves her armor as an offering at the Abbey of St. Denis. |
| Dec. 1429 | Joan is raised to the rank of nobility by Charles VII. |
| May 23, 1430 | Captured by Burgundian forces at Compiegne and imprisoned. |
| Nov. 21, 1430 | Ransomed to the English and imprisoned in Rouen. |

**1431**   Tried as a heretic by the Roman
Catholic church; recants at the
cemetery of Saint-Ouen; withdraws
her recantation and is burned at the
stake on May 30.

**1456**   Pope Calixtus III declares the 1431
verdict against Joan of Arc null and
void.

**1920**   Roman Catholic church admits Joan of
Arc to its catalog of saints and declares
May 30 her feast day.

# Glossary

**bastion**   a large wooden tower used to defend or attack a position

**Church Militant**   the Roman Catholic church and church officials on earth, as opposed to the Church Triumphant, which refers to God and all the saints in Heaven

**canonized**   officially recognized as a saint by the Church

**coronation**   the act or occasion of crowning, as of a king or queen

**court**   a king or queen and his or her officers, advisers, and, sometimes, family, who act as the governing body; also the residence of a king or queen

**courtiers**   members of the royal court

**dauphin**   the eldest son of the king of France

76

**disinherited**   deprived of legal or social rights or of previously held special privileges

**duchy**   the territory of a duke or duchess; a dukedom

**heretic**   a person who holds controversial opinions about established religious teachings

**martyr**   one who willingly accepts death as the penalty for refusing to renounce religious beliefs

**prophecy**   a prediction of something to come

**recant**   to withdraw a statement or belief

**regent**   one who rules a kingdom when the king or queen is absent or unable to rule

**scribe**   an official court secretary or clerk

**siege**   a military blockade of a city to force its inhabitants to surrender

**witch**   a person thought to have magical and usually evil powers

**wizard**   a man thought to have magical powers

# Index

Tracy Christopher graduated summa cum laude with a Bachelor of Arts degree in French and comparative literature from Washington University in St. Louis, Missouri. Ms. Christopher is a Ph.D. candidate at New York University and currently teaches French at the Dalton School in New York City.

## Picture Credits

The Bettmann Archive: frontis, pp. 6, 14, 18–19, 27, 30, 40, 44, 58, 68; Gary Tong: 33, 49